Swing Style

Fashions of the
1930s-1950s

Maureen Reilly

Schiffer Publishing Ltd®

4880 Lower Valley Road, Atglen, PA 19310 USA

Copyright © 2000 by Maureen Reilly
Library of Congress Catalog Card Number: 99-66076

Designed by Bonnie M. Hensley
Typeset in Bernard Fashion BT/Aldine721 BT

ISBN: 0-7643-1009-7
Printed in China
1 2 3 4

Published by Schiffer Publishing Ltd.
4880 Lower Valley Road
Atglen, PA 19310
Phone: (610) 593-1777; Fax: (610) 593-2002
E-mail: Schifferbk@aol.com
Please visit our website catalog at **www.schifferbooks.com**

In Europe, Schiffer books are distributed by Bushwood Books
6 Marksbury Avenue Kew Gardens
Surrey TW9 4JF England
Phone: 44 (0)208-392-8585; Fax: 44 (0)208-392-9876
E-mail: Bushwd@aol.com

This book may be purchased from the publisher.
·Include $3.95 for shipping. Please try your bookstore first.
We are interested in hearing from authors with book ideas on related subjects.
You may write for a free printed catalog.

This is for my husband, Rocky Saunders
. . . dedicated to the one I love.

Contents

Acknowledgments

This book would not have been possible without the support of my friends; Lis Normoyle with her shop *Luxe*; and Marlene Davenport with *Cheap Thrills*. (See also Vintage Resources Guide.) I could always count on them for encouragement and the generous loan of get-down vintage clothes for my many photo shoots. Speaking of which, a big thanks to John Klycinski, my long-time photographer in Benecia who shot several images — in addition to the work by Gideon Dominguez.

It was Gideon who introduced me to the *Just 4 Kids* agency in Sacramento, and the talented young models who really made this book come to life. We shot in studios, and at several hotel and restaurant locations: *The Inn at Benecia Bay* and *The Jefferson Street Mansion* in Benecia; *Vizcaya*, *Harlow's* and *A Shot of Class* in Sacramento.

Of course, we also photographed swing clothes in action at *Salazar Studios* in Sacramento. Many thanks to competition dance duo Ricardo Salazar and Christina Groves: they really made the point that dance clothing, vintage or not, must be designed to *move*. Finally, thanks to my long-time hairstylist and friend Art Cajigas at *Studio 28* in Sacramento, who put up with a last-minute request for 1940s updos on the models.

— I —
Opening Act

Swing is a dance craze sweeping this country, for the second time around. Essentially a modern dance, swing was born eight decades ago in the wake of World War I. The tempo of life quickened in the late twenties, jumping smart just to stay a pace ahead of changing social and political forces. Women shortened their skirts and flirted in public. With a reduced work week, men flirted back.

You Go, Goddess

During the teens and twenties, it was widely believed that theatrical dance had an elevating effect. The costumes favored by expressionist dancers like Isadore Duncan were styled after goddess togas from ancient Greece. Even genteel tea gowns were loose and flowing. Such clothing was not only artistic, but comfortable. Most importantly to our story, they allowed the ease of movement that is so essential for dancing.

Music and dance were a natural outlet for this new-found freedom, as ragtime gave birth to the blues. This was the Jazz Era, precursor to Swing. It was a uniquely American expression of bold and innovative music. The elements of early jazz have been traced to turn-of-the-century New Orleans where the musical heritage of French, Spanish and African cultures blended in the fields and rail yards, at the church and saloon, on the front porch and street corner.

Many New Orleans musicians were academically trained, but others could not even read — so the music developed with a strong element of improvisation. The rhythm of jazz is boisterous and uniquely alive, much like its cousin Ragtime. This was music for hard-working people to enjoy, in the mainstream of a melting pot society.

Ragtime emerged as a new musical form when the upright piano was invented. With its compact size, the upright brought the diverse musical range of a keyboard into a non-traditional venue. To put it bluntly, into the honky-tonk and bordello. Jazzmen would mock the uppercrust by *ragging* a tune, replacing a series of notes with one or placing syncopated accents where least expected.

I Got Rhythm

"Rhythm is the identifying phenomenon of jazz, but, as with the basic elements of any art, it is difficult to explain rhythm in terms of a precise chain of causes and effects. Rhythm in jazz is like rhythm in poetry or painting. [Now] we can enjoy the prodigious achievement of the jazz musicians who from the very beginning wove all the elements of their art — pitch, texture, melodic and harmonic organization — around the dominating force of rhythm."

Leonard Feather, Where Swing Came From, *The Swing Era* (1970) Time-Life Records.

A gauzy afternoon dress from the 1920s, worn by a graceful Donna Cherry. The hip bandeau is a delightful example of ribbonwork, hand-crafted in the same gauzy fabric. Value: $125.00. *Courtesy of It's About Time.*

TOMMY DORSEY

A very young Old Blue Eyes was a headliner vocalist for big bands in the 1940s, pictured here with Tommy Dorsey. Sinatra's vocal inflections had the rhythmic cadence of jazz.

Professional dancer, Ricardo Salazar, demonstrates how to go *flying home*.

The New Orleans style came to be known as Dixieland, a term that is now recognized to cover a variation of jazz with improvised swing elements. This new sound originally emigrated from New Orleans up and down the Mississippi River. By the early 1900s, the steamboat days memorialized by Mark Twain were over, although showboats continued to operate. They carried some passengers, and much entertainment, port- to-port. Some of the best early-generation jazz musicians played the boats — often to the lead of the gifted Fate Marable, whose eye for young talent spotted such notable sidemen as Louis Armstrong and Johnny Dodds.

Musicians worked the boats not only because they needed the pay, but as a way to reach new audiences. Many settled in Chicago, which became home to the Original Dixieland Jazz Band in 1916. The following year, ODJB made the first jazz record ever issued, in 72-rpm from Victor. Sales of the record skyrocketed, with eventually more than a million copies sold. Its success led Columbia to press the second ODJB recording of two songs that still make up the lexicon of jazz: *Darktown Strutter's Ball* and *Indiana*.

The Early Platters

"With these recordings began the central history of American jazz, which has found on records its place, its forms, its style, its major features, its lifeblood, its identity. The confines of the 10-inch, 72-rpm record became to jazz what the sonnet was to the poetry of the Italian, French and English Renaissance. The short-playing shellac disk fixed the form on which jazz was to make its most notable statements from the ODJB recordings in 1917 until the emergence, in 1948, of the 33 long-playing record.

Not only did the limitations of records force the musicians to express a lot of good ideas in a short time, but the wide dissemination of these ideas that recordings made possible stimulated the development of jazz. Musicians thousands of miles apart could listen to and learn from each other."

Leonard Feather, Where Swing Came From, *The Swing Era* (1970) Time-Life Records.

In the mid-1920s, with the strong influence of Chicago sidemen like Louis Armstrong, jazz changed from an ensemble style to a sophisticated blend of group and soloist. From the beginning, as second trumpet behind Joe Oliver, Armstrong had a solo presence that seemed to shine without effort. His control and precision were beyond the technical ability of most other performers. Decades later, playing with *The Hot Five*, he toured Europe and helped bring swing to an international audience. From Louis Armstrong's wide mouth, which earned him the nickname "Satchelmouth" or "Satchmo," would emit the greatest of jazz growls. Following his husky lead, other sidemen shouted out rattles and grunts. This is to singing, what *Salt Peanuts* is to caviar.

Another lasting influence came from the golden cornet of Leon Bismarck "Bix" Beiderbecke. He grew up admiring New Orleans musicians on the Mississippi showboats passing by his hometown of Davenport, Iowa. Bix played a sweet melodic line with strong personal style, but his talent lay in the ability to re-work classical music with a jazz inflection. Although he died of pneumonia in 1931, Bix became a jazz legend when his short life was penned by Dorothy Baker in *Young Man with a Horn*.

Lindy Charleston

The original Charleston was one of the first fast dances to emerge from the Jazz Age. As stock prices rose in the 1920s, so did skirts. Female legs were on display for the first time in history, with knees rouged by the daring flappers. The new style of dress allowed freedom of movement, and fresh young things were soon doing crazy dances. By the late 1930s, the Charleston had blended with Lindy Hop moves. Just a few years later, the energetic Lindy was the dance of choice for young *hepcats*.

Swing it, sister. Shellet Smallwood shows off a swirly print dress from the early 1940s. Value: $75.00. *Courtesy of Luxe*.

Paul Whiteman was known as the King of Jazz.

In Chicago, during the mid-1920s, Paul Whiteman's showmanship, and ability to blend classical music with improvisations, helped make jazz respectable. At the same time, that toddling town watched a teen-age Benny Goodman debut on the clarinet, and saw Glenn Miller polish his arranging talents.

New York soon became a mecca for jazz musicians, with its heart in Harlem. There, in the Savoy Hotel Ballroom, true swing was born in the late 1920s. This was during the Harlem Renaissance that gave the first rich expression to black culture in America. The society swells flocked to *The Cotton Club* where Duke Ellington, Cab Calloway and Fats Waller held court.

Stompin' at the Savoy takes on new meaning with the tale of a reporter's query to Shorty George Snowden on the hotel dance floor. Asked what to call the new steps, he replied: "Why it's Lindy's Hop, man." The name stuck, as did his namesake dance step the "Shorty George." Swing dancing is still classified today as the Lindy Hop along with its tamer cousins: East Coast, West Coast, Western and Shag.

By 1929, Frankie Manning was providing choreography for a group of Harlem kids who had formed the original Whitey's Lindy Hoppers.

The group, assembled by a fight promoter who knew talent with feet as well as fists, performed in elegant dance clubs in this country and abroad for many years. Manning, age 85, still teaches the steps he helped create, from a Los Angeles dance studio.

Just move your feet; you'll look good if the girl is sweet. Derek Gouveia woos a sunshine miss, Nakita Keitt. The cotton house-dress is mid-1930s (sun hat is not vintage). Value: $25.00. *Courtesy of It's About Time.*

The Depression caused the crash of many jazz clubs in New York and Chicago. However, jazz played on in Kansas City, where the faithful were still flush with profits from bootleg booze. K.C. favored a heavy, driving beat with a strong blues back — as befits a roustabout town. At its worst, it was more noise than rhythm; at its best, it was irresistible dance music, and it helped transform jazz into the new sound of swing, growling sidemen and all.

The progression to swing speeded up thanks to the popularity of strong blues singers like Ella Fitzgerald and Billie Holliday; or those who used a jazz backup, like the Mills Brothers and Bing Crosby.

In 1935, the public couldn't stop humming a catchy tune called *The Music Goes 'Round and Around*. This ditty was recorded by trumpeter Eddy Farley and trombonist Mike Riley with the Onyx Club Band in New York City, attributed to an arrangement by Duke Ellington and his songwriting partner Billy Smallwood. The blithe spirit of this song has become recognized as the anthem of our nation's Swing Era.

Lady Sings the Blues

Billie Holliday has been called the last true jazz singer. As faithfully portrayed by Diana Ross in the movie *Lady Sings the Blues*, a teen-age Billie began singing in Harlem, where she eventually launched her career from the Cotton Club. Later, she was a vocalist for Count Basie's band. Her unmistakable bittersweet sound came from a technique of subtly altering the melody by placing notes just before or after the beat.

The music goes around and around with this Martin Alto Sax. Shaped and chased in solid silver during the 1940s, it's the same brand and vintage favored by many jazz soloists today.

A radiant Billie Holliday at the height of her popularity in the mid-1940s. Her smart white suit sets off the signature camellias in her hair. During the war years, women dressed up their work-a-day suits for a night on-the-town.

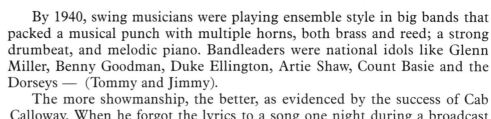

By 1940, swing musicians were playing ensemble style in big bands that packed a musical punch with multiple horns, both brass and reed; a strong drumbeat, and melodic piano. Bandleaders were national idols like Glenn Miller, Benny Goodman, Duke Ellington, Artie Shaw, Count Basie and the Dorseys — (Tommy and Jimmy).

The more showmanship, the better, as evidenced by the success of Cab Calloway. When he forgot the lyrics to a song one night during a broadcast from the Cotton Club, his improvisation launched the evergreen crowd-pleasing *Hi De Ho*. Just behind the bandleaders in popularity were the vocalists, many of whom went on to star in movies after the Swing Era. Girl vocalists like Kate Smith, Ella Fitzgerald, Doris Day, Lena Horne and the Hutton Sisters wore pretty gowns and sang pretty low-down.

Top: Big bandleader Artie Shaw.

Bottom: Benny Goodman and his "licorice stick."

Cab Calloway zoots it up in the 1970s, for the album cover of a reissued *Minnie the Moocher* and other *Hi-de-hi-de-hi-de-Ho* hits.

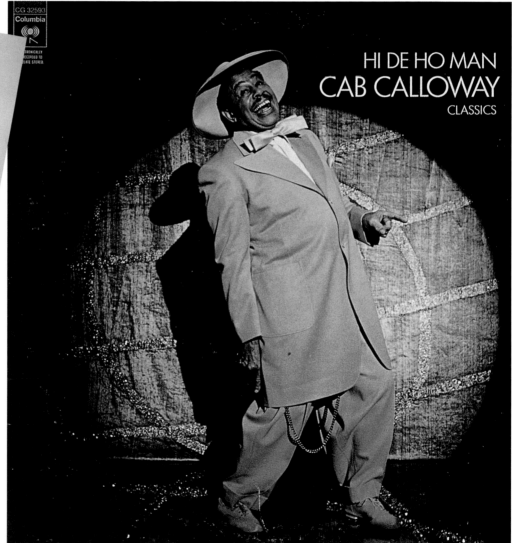

HI DE HO MAN
CAB CALLOWAY
CLASSICS

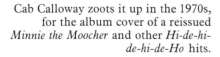

Doris Day began her career as a girl vocalist, shown here with Les Brown and his Band of Reknown. Gotta love those fingerless gloves!

The venue is *A Shot of Class*, a Sacramento supper club that has offered ballroom and swing for the past 15 years. Owner Georgia Cazimier was inspired by the stories her parents told of dance dates in her namesake state. The girl vocalist is played by Elizabeth Haskett, making her debut in a 1930s black satin gown trimmed in turquoise cloth and shot with silver. Value, dress: $45.00 — $65.00. *Author's Collection*.

With America's entrance into World War II the band members enlisted, but their music played on. It could be heard blaring forth from radios and jukeboxes, even on the war front. At base canteens and USO dances, men and women in uniform beat their feet eight-to-the-bar with swinging classics like *Boogie Woogie Bugle Boy From Company C*.

The debonair Duke Ellington tickles the ivories for a group of servicemen on leave at a special gig in New York City, circa 1944.

Dance for joy anytime, anywhere. This parking lot lift is by Matt Huey, in a *retro* gray flannel suit and vintage straw Fedora. His partner is Katie Harris, in a 1930s rayon day dress (the whimsical print shows racing horses). Value, Fedora: $45.00. *Courtesy of It's About Time*. Value, dress: $15.00 — $25.00. *Author's collection*.

Don't sit under the apple tree with anyone else but me. This obligatory warning from a departing serviceman was made famous by Glenn Miller, as re-enacted here by Jennifer Domser. Apple-red ottoman fabric gives this dress substance; black silk braiding lends charm. By Peggy Hunt, a California designer, circa 1945. Value $55.00 — $65.00. *Author's collection.*

Swing was still strong on V-E Day, for tattooed types like Matt Huey, with date Ashley Anderson. (Her dress is actually circa 1955; by *Marion McCoy*; it features a Chantilly lace bodice studded with rhinestones.) Value: $45.00 — $55.00. *Courtesy of Cheap Thrills.*

Glenn Miller, young and handsome in the late 1930s. Some years later when America entered the war, he tried to enlist in the Navy but was turned down as being over age! Fortunately, the Army recognized his potential as a leader of men and bands.

With V-E Day and V-J Day came a public outcry for a return to normalcy. Out went the ration books and man-tailored clothing; in came new appliances, big cars, and the ultra-feminine "New Look." One thing remained constant, which was the popularity of modern dance in its athletic expression of swing style.

Throughout America's involvement in World War II there was a government ban on recording, which put a stalemate on new swing sounds. But even though new records were not pressed, ensembles and vocalists buoyed our boys overseas.

Glenn Miller's Mood

Glenn Miller flavored his arrangements with sweet reed voicing from a clarinet lead. He also pioneered the "call and response" between horns after enlarging the brass section in his big band at Glen Island Casino in New Rochelle. This was in 1939, following several unsuccessful starts — but from that point on, Miller's career skyrocketed. The next year his recording of *Tuxedo Junction* sold 115,000 copies in its first week of issue. In 1942, Miller enlisted in the Army, and was commissioned as Director of Bands for the Air Corps. He toured military bases overseas, playing up to 17 gigs a week. Miller died on a military transport flight, just weeks before the war ended.

The tempo of life had changed. For a variety of seemingly unrelated reasons, such as Glenn Miller's tragic death, most big bands had dispersed by the mid-1950s. Of course, swing music has been revived several times since then, hence the inspiration for this book!

Hoppin' with Hamp

Lionel Hampton's career soared when he experimented on the vibes at a studio session for Louis Armstrong in 1930, and they made the first recording of this new musical instrument. A drummer until then, Hampton had found his instrument at age 21. Four years later, he formed his own band and, by 1978, he won jazz acclaim for his one-millionth performance of *Flying Home*. Hampton credits his skills to early musical instruction by Sister Peters at the Holy Rosary Academy in Wisconsin – rather an unlikely training ground! "So now I got a chance to play drums and this sister was our teacher. Boy, was she great, too. She was hard on you – if you didn't play those paradiddles right, she'd take those sticks and break your knuckles."

The crowds went crazy for Lionel Hampton's vibrant vibes style, inspiring the best in Lindy Hoppers.

17

It was in the early 1950s that teenagers were recognized as a discrete population for the first time. Looking back at this decade, through the haze of fond nostalgia, life seemed like one long dance party for the teeny bopping crowd. At malt shops and diners across small-town America, teens held impromptu sock hops to the happy sound of a jukebox.

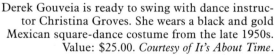

Derek Gouveia is ready to swing with dance instructor Christina Groves. She wears a black and gold Mexican square-dance costume from the late 1950s. Value: $25.00. *Courtesy of It's About Time.*

This was also the era of high school promenades, a variation on coming-out parties hitherto, reserved for debutante daughters of the rich and privileged. Now every girl could be a Cinderella in frothing chiffon and cascading corsage, until the clock struck curfew on prom night.

Satin Dolls

The 1930s debutante ball was a precursor to the 1950s prom. In that era, debs wore bias-cut gowns with smocked and tucked detailing, swinging to Duke Ellington's classic *Satin Doll*. Of course, satin remained popular for prom night, and any other fancy occasions in the decades that followed.

This rose-pink frock with its tucked and bowed bodice, might have been worn by a 1930s miss at one of the many cotillions that would have preceded her actual debut. Value: $45.00 — $65.00. *Courtesy of It's About Time.*

A celadon-green gown, elegant enough for the biggest cotillion of the season. It was probably made-to-order by a wealthy socialite, whose excellent taste is reflected in the pared-down design. Note the self-fabric inset, which helps define the curve of a bias-cut skirt. Value: $75.00. *Courtesy of It's About Time*.

In the 1960s and 1970s, the joyous sound of swing gave way to the dissonance of acid rock, and the distraction of disco. Today, as we enter a new millennium, the music pendulum is swinging back. All across America small bands are reviving Big Band tunes, as a new generation learns to jump smart!

Tommy Dorsey enjoyed a long career after his split from brother Jimmy. He's pictured here on the album cover of a 1970s release.

Weave a web of romance in this wonderful turquoise moiré cocktailer from the 1950s with its spiderweb of soutache, rhinestones and pearls. Value: $45.00. *Author's collection.*

The trombone was one of several brass horns that put jive into the Big Band sound. Seen taking a break from her jam session, Elizabeth Haskett relaxes in a comfy cotton day dress from the 1940s. Value: $25.00. *Author's collection.*

The Swing Era

The years 1935 — 1942 marked the Swing Era. The Big Bands buoyed the hopes of an American population just emerging from the Depression, only to breathe the distant fumes of World War II. Girls wore cotton house-dresses to dance the Lindy Hop on street corners in Harlem, a two-step away from *The Cotton Club* where wealthy ladies in satin swooned to Duke Ellington's *Black and Tan Fantasy*.

Dance Tunes

At right: Jamie Bradham wears a 1930s printed lawn house-dress with rhinestone *jelly* buttons. At left: On Kristi Talbert, a similar sundress from the 1950s. Value, each: $35.00 — $45.00. *Courtesy of Cheap Thrills.*

On hot August nights, kids gathered in each other's living rooms and danced to the radio or record player. They kept cool with electric fans and iced drinks, as in this rather liberal re-creation of a Depression-era dance date.

The uppercrust danced the night away at swank night-clubs like the legendary *El Morocco* in New York City. From an advertisement in February 1946.

Crepe Connection

On Andrea Pritchard, a fuchsia crepe dress sparked with sequins on the self-belt. Value: $55.00 — $75.00. *Courtesy of Lottie Ballou.*

Rebecca Nuttall wears a grape crepe dinner dress with lattice detail, circa 1945. Value: $55.00 — $75.00. *Courtesy of Lottie Ballou.*

"New Angle on Dresses." Two views of a dolman-sleeved dress with oversize patch pockets, in moss green. The wine design stands alone. Offered by *McCalls Patterns* in 1949.

Midnight blue brightened by a field of sequin flowers. At its side, black and pink meet to good advantage in a side-draped crepe. Both were advertised in October 1947.

Opposite page: Katie Harris sizzles in a cool 1940s aqua crepe with steel-beaded bodice. Matt Huey sports a necktie belt, in the manner of Fred Astaire. Value, dress: $45.00 — $65.00. *Courtesy of Cheap Thrills.*

Beauty on the Bias

A glowing russet bias-cut satin dance dress. The zipper closure in back ends at a big bow, forming a mock bustle (not shown). Value: $55.00 — $75.00. *Author's collection.*

Opposite page:
Bottom left: A pretty pink crepe with mock bustle, as advertised in February 1946.

Opposite page: This sapphire-blue silk dress, with tucked peplum and portrait collar, was surely a jewel in someone's wardrobe circa 1945. Value: $45.00 — $65.00. *Courtesy of It's About Time.*

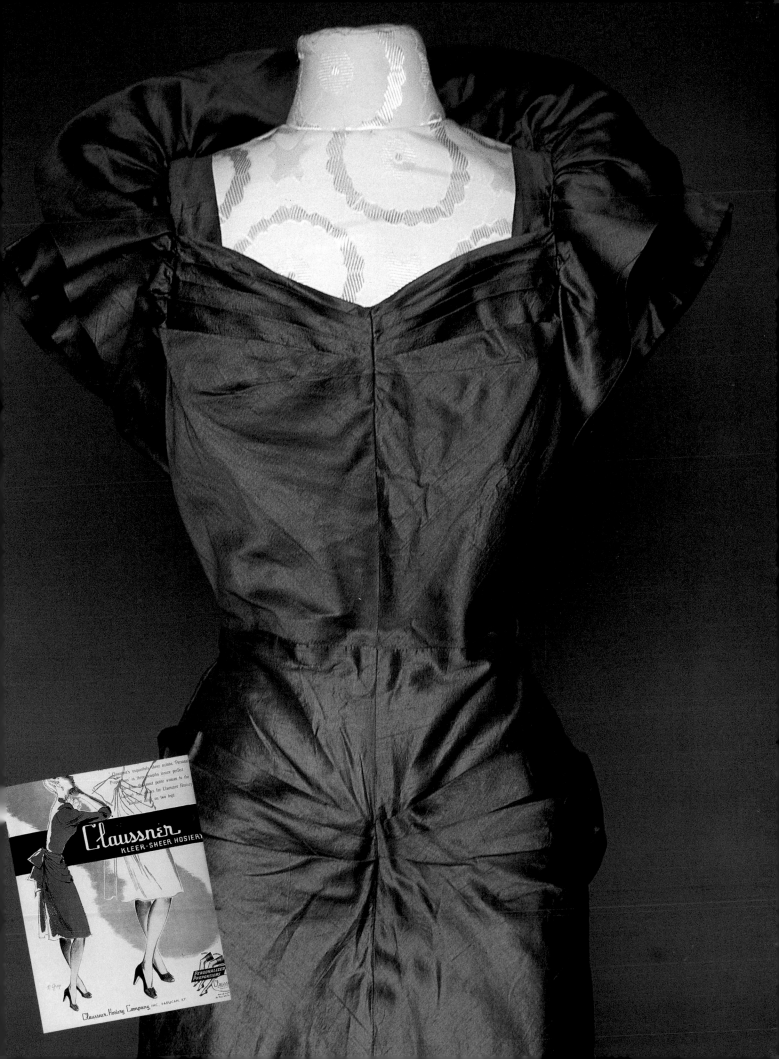

Lindsey Province preens in bias-cut black satin with draped bows at shoulder and hip. Value: $55.00 — $75.00. *Courtesy of It's About Time.*

From top Hollywood designer Howard Greer,
dress with striped top and mock peplum
married to a black skirt, for a separates look.
As advertised in March 1946.

Crepe dress with a side drape. The
slashed bodice boasts a modesty panel
with the glow of a rose corsage. By Jo
Copeland for *Patullo*, as advertised in
March 1946.

Two black beauties offered by *Fred
Greenberg* in September 1948. Each
dress has a side drape, but the neck-
lines vary (jewel and keyhole).

This *William Barr* mock peplum dress sold
at *Montaldo's* department store in 1946.

Parisian charm is evident in a black
wool crepe dress. From *La Femme
Chic*, Spring 1942.

An afternoon dress by couturier
Marcelle Alix with a crystal-pleated,
tiered skirt. As seen in *Album de Figaro*,
Spring 1947.

The side pleat is a kick; the slashed
bodice is a tease (notice the frilly *fichu*).
As offereded by *Fred Greenberg* in 1946.

A rayon crepe dress, graced with a side ruffle in
rayon taffeta. By Jo Copeland for *Patullo*, as
advertised in February 1946.

Two views of a two-toned and side-draped crepe dress,
advertised in September 1946. The Beefeater hat is a
reference to medieval style, then enjoying a brief revival.

Mock aprons and color-blocked fabric made fashion news in the
1940s. Both devices are used to good effect in a crepe dance
dress. By *Charles Armour*, as advertised in February 1946.

Dramatic by Design

A pair of after-five
dresses, identical but
for color. In black and
red rayon crepe, they
were custom-ordered
by a prominent Los
Angeleno in the 1940s.
Value, each: $85.00 —
$105.00. *Courtesy of
Lottie Ballou.*

The Hollywood designer Adrian was often copied, and this spectacular color-blocked cocktail dress helped start a national trend. Value: Special. *Courtesy of Luxe.*

An evening dress by Adrian at his most dramatic, as advertised in February 1951.

Coco Chanel launched her career in the early 1920s with a long sweater that featured a *trompe l'oiel* white bow. Her trick was reprised in this 1940s dress with *faux* bow outlined in pink sequins on black crepe. Value: $55.00 — $75.00. *Courtesy of Lottie Ballou.*

Swing it on
home, in this
black silk
cocktail dress
with bodice of
red brocade,
circa 1950. Value:
$45.00. *Courtesy
of It's About Time*.

A gala gown for dinner and dancing circa 1948, when Paris dictated a revival of the Regency look. As worn by Lisa Heigher at the *Vizcaya* bed-and-breakfast in Sacramento, this gown was custom-ordered by its original owner with great attention to detail. The stripes are not printed, but hand-sewn from turquoise and black silk. Value: $105 — $125.00. *Courtesy of Lottie Ballou.*

Drama from the designer Dorothy O'Hara, whose after-five dresses were puckered with precision. The dress and straw boater are both mid-1940s; the rhinestone jewelry is early 1950s. Worn by Elizabeth Haskett at *The Jefferson Street Mansion* in Benecia. Value, dress: $45.00 — $65.00. *Courtesy of Cheap Thrills.*

Skull caps like this were the height of chic in the 1930s, as modeled here by Linda Stokes. Studs were also liberally pronged into dresses, as in her two-piece black rayon. Value, hat: $25.00. Value, dress: $55.00 — $75.00. *Courtesy of It's About Time*.

Brass studs and other medieval accents made a bold fashion statement in the mid 1930s and 1940s, as styled on Kristi Talbert. Value, dress: $45.00. *Courtesy of Cheap Thrills.*

Although this two-piece knit is not vintage, it shows great Art Deco style. The black and white chevrons blend well with the 1930s décor at *Harlow's* in Sacramento, where swing dance is enjoying a revival. Value: $55.00. *Courtesy of Luxe.*

Opposite page: A felt circle skirt with three-dimensional flowers, circa 1950. By Juli Lynne Charlot , who is credited with designing the first poodle skirt! Worn by Elizabeth Haskett at *Harlow's* in Sacramento. Value: $35.00 — $55.00. *Author's collection.*

A linen sheath matched to its own cotton voile jumper. The sheer pleated skirt flips in front and back, for dance ease. By Anne Fogarty, circa 1960. Wear it with a silly necklace like this, with dangling perfume bottles. Value, dress: $45.00. *Author's collection.*

Basic Black

Black rayon is cut on the bias and tucked into a peplum, for cocktails circa 1945. Jazz it up now, as then, with a set of *faux* opals and rubies. Value, dress: $45.00. *Author's collection.*

On Lisa Steele, even a cocktail dress looks angelic. In sheer rayon crepe, circa 1940 — with a trio of rhinestone clips rolling along the collar. Value: $45.00 — $65.00. *Courtesy of Lottie Ballou.*

Preening before the mirror, Elizabeth Haskett wears a black rayon crepe dress (not vintage). Her turquoise bird-of-paradise hat swoops stylishly in back. Value, dress: $35.00. *Author's collection.*

Bead-dazzling Black

It's the berries! A fabulous black crepe cocktail dress with strawberries strewn across the shoulders, from *Eisenberg*, circa 1945. These berries are hand-sewn from red sequins and yellow glass beads — good enough to eat, by model Lindsay Province. Value: $75.00 — $95.00. *Author's collection*.

The little black dress in rayon crepe circa 1945, as worn by Jennifer Domser. Multicolor sequins brighten the bodice like an oversized corsage. Value, dress: $35.00 — $45.00. *Courtesy of Cheap Thrills.*

Swing it, in black linen tucked at the hip and beaded at the pockets, circa 1945. Wrap it in a sharkskin scarf, like model Rebecca Nuttall. Value, dress: $45.00. *Author's collection.*

Andrea Pritchard dazzles in a black dress with floral fireworks, circa 1942. She graces the bar at *Harlow's* in Sacramento. Value: $55.00 — $65.00. *Courtesy of Cheap Thrills.*

Beautiful hand-sewn beadwork makes this mid-1940s cocktail dress special, and the grosgrain turban makes it swing, on model Lisa Steele. Value, dress: $55.00 — $75.00. *Courtesy of Lottie Ballou.* Value, hat: $35.00. *Author's collection.*

Shellet Smallwood and Derek Gouveia flirt to beat the band! She's in vintage black crepe with sequin trim, he's in a revival Fedora. Her sequined belt was hand-sewn in the early 1940s. Value, dress with belt: $55.00 — $65.00. *Courtesy of Cheap Thrills*.

Sunny Daze

Like peonies from heaven, a sunny cotton house-dress with self-sash and big red wooden button, circa 1932. Value: $15.00 — $25.00. *Courtesy of Lottie Ballou.*

A cotton day dress with perky pleats in back, from the late 1930s. The fantasy print, in a bold South-of-the-Border motif, keeps this home-made style from being *homely*. Value: $35.00 — $55.00. *Courtesy of Lottie Ballou.*

At the Improv

Mixing modern and vintage clothing creates wardrobe synergy. If you're not comfortable with the idea of wearing someone else's dress, or you can't find a period outfit in your size, or you're afraid of ripping the seams in a favorite vintage piece – create your own mix 'n match look with new 'n old items.

A rayon house dress in brilliant purple, punctuated with faceted black buttons. In the 1940s this dress did chores; today, it goes to the ball. Value: $25.00. *Author's collection.*

The dress is really a modern stretch-knit skirt, worn like a bustier. It gains vintage style with a satin bed jacket from the 1930s, and a rosy halo hat from the same era. Value, jacket: $15.00. *Courtesy of It's About Time.*

Day dresses had great style 50 years ago! Case in point, a pastel rayon gabardine with oversized pockets and dramatic button, as advertised in February 1946. Wear it today, with black patent sandals and a chunky bangle bracelet.

Sun lovers of 1936, in shorts and separates styled for the beach and tennis court. Look for the original version of these playsuits, or style a modern jumper with vintage *panache*.

The diagonal stripes on this rope-tied cotton skirt are hand-painted. It's the type of luxury detail that drives thrifty shoppers to vintage stores. Shown with a wrap shell and ballet flats, timeless in style. As advertised by the *J.W. Robinson* department store in March 1946.

More fun beach togs from the late 1930s. These shortalls, pajama pants, halter tops and shorts still look up-to-the-minute and breathing life into the adage: Form follows function.

A cotton sundress by *Kate Weill* with scallop border on the cover-up. As advertised in February 1946.

You're the Tops

Just a sweet cotton voile blouse circa 1950, to wear with jeans or a circle skirt. Red dots and dashes are smocked across the bodice. Value: $15.00. *Courtesy of Cheap Thrills*.

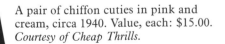

A pair of chiffon cuties in pink and cream, circa 1940. Value, each: $15.00. *Courtesy of Cheap Thrills*.

At the Improv

Can't find a vintage outfit that's just right for you? Look for a beaded sweater, style it with *any* skirt or slacks. For footwear add ballet flats, retro sandals or sexy mules and you're ready to dance!

Gold-threaded organza blouses were worn with lacy camisoles in the 1940s. Layer them over thin cotton tank-tops, today. Value, each: $15.00 — $25.00. *Courtesy of Cheap Thrills.*

Two fabulous suit jackets in new-old stock from the late 1930s. One still bears the original hangtag: *Junior Fashions by Carole King.* The red ottoman fabric is trimmed in black chenille, with jet beading and gold braiding in the Spanish manner. The green faille boasts a rayon jungle-print inset at each shoulder, as a surrealistic touch. Value, each: $55.00. *Courtesy of It's About Time.*

Hand-beaded cardigans were all the rage in the 1950s, typically imported from Hong Kong. Paired with a new lace skirt. Value: $45.00 — $65.00. *Author's collection.*

Top left: Coral jewelry was hot, as seen in this magazine illustration from 1955.

Top Center & Bottom: Two vintage sweaters are paired with retro cotton sundresses. One is hand-beaded in gold and bronze glass on black wool; the other is strewn with hand-sewn branch coral on cream cashmere. Value, each: $45.00 — $65.00. *Author's collection.*

Well-Suited

An abstract print suit as advertised by the classy I. Magnin department store in February 1946.

The *Lilli Ann Corp.* of San Francisco specialized in suits and coats in the 1940s and 1950s. Styling details, like this triple-tier peplum advertised in October 1953, make the label highly collectible. For swing, wear this type of tight jacket with a modern stretch-fabric skirt or slacks.

A black rayon suit sprigged with pink carnations, circa 1950. It's the very picture of springtime, on model Jamie Bradham. Value: $55.00 — $75.00. *Courtesy of It's About Time.*

Prints Please ———

A cotton little-evening dress from the mid-1930s, sweet and simple on Elizabeth Haskett. The abstract print is amusingly modern. Value: $55.00. *Courtesy of It's About Time.*

BOUFFANT OR SHEATH

In 1938, *McCalls Patterns* recommended a splashy floral print for this swingy evening dress. It was shown with a slim companion dress in turquoise, with draped fullness in back.

Be cool and chic in this side-draped rayon after-five dress. Turquoise and gray were a popular color combo in the early 1950s. The velour boater, banded in tulle, is from the 1940s. Value, dress: $45.00 — $65.00. *Courtesy of Lottie Ballou.*

59

Exotic orchids are printed on brown crepe. From the 1940s, but just right for today's Jane of the Urban Jungle, as shown by Andrea Pritchard. Value, dress: $45.00 — $55.00. *Courtesy of Lottie Ballou.*

Cherries Jubilee circa 1945, on Rebecca Nuttall. The *millefiore* dress is cotton lawn, banded in black silk ribbon at sleeves and peplum. Value, dress: $45.00 — $65.00. *Courtesy of Lottie Ballou.*

A silky shirt-dress with swingy skirt; the silly print of storefronts is pure 1950s. Value: $25.00 — $35.00. *Courtesy of Cheap Thrills.*

The Chinoiserie print gives interest to this pleated shirt-waist from the early 1950s. Value: $25.00 — $35.00. *Courtesy of Lottie Ballou.*

Men could wear the prints, too. A great selection of *Bali Cay* styles as advertised by Arrow Shirts in 1932. Readers were urged: *Put some romance in your loaf life!*

Put some romance in your loaf life!

ARROW
Bali Cay

There's nothing shy about this hothouse flower,
blooming on rayon in colors nature can only envy.
This 1940s dress is worn with modern attitude, by
Kristi Talbert. Value, dress: $35.00 — $45.00.
Courtesy of Lottie Ballou.

A flock of frocks from *McCalls Patterns*
showing *More Color* for Spring 1938.
Prints were popular, especially when
mixed with a bolero for versatility.

Opposite page: To the modern eye,
some of the abstract prints from the
1940s look like drapery fabric. Either
way, the effect is charming, as worn by
Monica Moreno. Value: $35.00 —
$55.00. *Courtesy of It's About Time.*

Classic 1940s style in a fantasy rayon print; the squared neckline is perfect for clips. Elizabeth Haskett wears it with a doll hat of cellophane straw, from the same era. Value, dress: $55.00 — $75.00. *Courtesy of Lottie Ballou.*

Dress companies often revise old clothing styles, termed *retro* as distinct from *vintage*. When you find one you like, snap it up! These clothes have the convenience of modern washing instructions and sizing. Another advantage is that retro clothing can be worn with carefree abandon, safe in the knowledge that a delicate vintage garment is not at risk. If you find a retro dress, or choose to have one custom-made by a specialty store, you can still jazz it up with authentic accessories!

This retro rayon print dress features a mock peplum, in true 1940s style. The dress gains period grace with a vintage halo hat, inspiring flirtation by Matt Huey and Ashley Anderson. Value, hat: $25.00 — $45.00. *Author's collection.*

Pretty faces peer out from the black background of a *Jr. Guild* dress from 1946.

This luncheon costume is a nice study in contrasts, with a traditional blouse updated by a fantasy *macquillage* print. Quite the hot number with a matching print hat, as advertised in February 1946.

AFTERNOON IN COLOUR

For many seasons now, it has been smugly satisfying to wear discreet black for afternoon; to spice it with more or less astonishing hats or jewellery made for conversation. This year the spectrum changes. Black is still there, of course; and here and everywhere. But you may feel too safe, a little dull, if you turn your back on colour in the afternoon. There is a fresh feeling that runs through all the good collections ... a feeling for pretty dresses; some of the prettiest are in colour. You will see them under mink, or Persian, or nutria. A blue like the one on this page; a new rosy wine; a worldly smoky green; a cheerful geranium. The lines are unfussed, self-contained; often long-sleeved, high-necked. Colour gives the key ... obvious intent to please.

This bubbly sundress with its lemon-lime print is by *Connie Foster* of California, as advertised for resort wear in December 1945.

Another version of the resort sundress circa 1945, in classy black polka dots from *Ben Reig*. Still great for swinging summer nights, a half-century later.

Capri pants were hot in the 1940s, and revived several times since. This fashionable version features a side-swiped bow; swing it with a sexy halter top, and strappy sandals.

Tunic dressing was still a strong fashion statement in January 1951. Shown in pleated blue silk sprinkled with springtime daisies, this dress would swirl — with the surprise of a straight skirt beneath.

The tunic dress was *tres chic* in the mid-1940s, as were bold prints adapted from fine art. This abstract floral design shows the influence of Miro, in ready-to-wear by *Herbert Sondheim*.

A sensational silk print gown from the early 1940s, casually styled with a deep V-neckline and handkerchief hem. Wear vintage gowns like this with retro wedge-heeled sandals.

This ad for *Quadriga Cloth* shows the whimsical side of 1940s prints, with scenes of children at play on a flaring hoe-down skirt.

Winkler's advertised its new line for Spring 1946 with quilted fields of country cotton prints. This fabric was typically made into sundresses and full skirts.

— 3 —
Postwar Changes

Pretty in Pink

During the war, boys in the band became men in uniform. On the homefront, the musical scene consisted of small bands and girl vocalists, or oldie-but-goodie platters, since there was a government restriction on new recordings. Soon after the war, the Big Bands dispersed. A notable exception was Woody Herman and the Thundering Herd, which recorded many of its greatest hits in the late 1940s and 1950s.

For other swing musicians, the postwar years were a time of innovation when some of the greatest sidemen experimented with new techniques. Before rock 'n roll was here to stay, hepcats were swinging to jazz combos in nightclubs and dance halls. Their younger counterparts were be-bopping at the corner *sweet shoppe*, where two bits put three platters on the jukebox.

A flattering fuchsia dress from the early 1960s, by *Tres Gay* of California. The ruffled hem really swings! Value: $25.00 — $35.00. *Courtesy of It's About Time*.

Sing *Summertime* with a blue note in this watermelon-pink sundress of lightweight denim. By *Pat Hartley of California*, with color-blocked hem and matching bolero. Value: $25.00. *Author's collection*.

Opposite page: Christina Groves shows the early classical training that led to her success in competitive swing dancing. This cotton-candy taffeta dress, with boatneck and bows, is from the late 1950s. Value: $35.00. *Author's collection*.

What could be more feminine than a frilly gown of blush-pink Chantilly lace? Christina Groves wears it to show off ballroom style with dance partner Ricardo Salazar. Value: $25.00 — $45.00. *Courtesy of It's About Time.*

Chantilly lace, and a pretty face...Make the world go 'round and 'round... So sang the **Big Bopper** in the 1950s; so dance Ricardo and Christina, today.

The Cocktail Hour

This linen shift is trimmed with soutache in the same shade of robins-egg blue, and shot with rhinestones for after-five sparkle. From the elegant *City of Paris* department store in San Francisco, circa 1957. Value: $25.00 — $45.00. *Courtesy of It's About Time.*

A strapless dress in black confetti-print tulle, circa 1955. It's trimmed in velvet and swathed in its own slim stole. Value: $15.00 — $25.00. *Courtesy of Cheap Thrills.*

Two views of strapless glamour from the mid-1950s. Each gown has a self-stole to chase away spring breezes.

A girl can really twirl in black crepe, with chartreuse satin at the peek-a-boo bodice and slip. Value: $35.00 — $55.00. *Courtesy of Cheap Thrills.*

Kiss me quick! A brocade and satin prom dress from the 1950s with sexy halter neckline. Value: $45.00 — $55.00. *Courtesy of Cheap Thrills.*

The mid-1950s cocktailer is delightful in *Mood Indigo* taffeta with a tiered full skirt and cuffed bracelet-length sleeves. Value: $45.00 — $65.00. *Courtesy of Cheap Thrills.*

Christina Groves is a red-hot vision, in velvet by *Suzy Perette* circa 1955. Value: $15.00 — $25.00. *Author's collection.*

A tiered skirt tinkles like a bell, in time for the cocktail hour. From a 1946 advertisement.

Who would expect such a classy number from *Frederick's of Hollywood?* In clingy red jersey with rose trim, circa 1975. Value: $25.00 — $45.00. *Courtesy of Trixie's Vintage Boutique.*

S'wonderful to dance the night away in red velvet! From a 1950s album cover for a re-release of Big Band music.

Champagne bubbles on a taffeta frock from the mid-1950s, worn by Ashley Anderson at *A Shot of Class* in Sacramento. Value: $35.00 — $45.00. *Courtesy of It's About Time.*

Opposite page, bottom: Monica Moreno is ready to spend some green, in a chiffon date dress with tiered skirt. By *Miss Elliette*, circa 1970. *Courtesy of Cherry*.

Fringe is always "in" as demonstrated by Elizabeth Haskett. Black crepe sheath by *Dress Towne*, circa 1975. Value: $45.00 — $65.00. *Courtesy of It's About Time*.

Red Roses for a Blue Lady. This silk-screened shantung cocktail dress sold at the I. Magnin & Co. department store, circa 1960. Value: $35.00 — $45.00. *Courtesy of Cheap Thrills*.

Be a Hawaiian siren in this 1950s strapless sarong with matching stole, worn with a traditional flower by Nakita Keitt. Value: $65.00 — $85.00. *Courtesy of Luxe*.

The balloon skirt by designer Nettie Rosenstein, as advertised in Spring 1951.

Nettie Rosenstein

French couturier Balenciaga popularized the balloon skirt in the late 1950s. This perky copycat is in a polished cotton print. Value: $45.00 — $55.00. *Courtesy of Luxe.*

For cocktails on the veranda or swing dancing under a summer sky — wear a lettuce-green cotton organdy halter dress, like this one from 1951.

In Spring 1951, couturier Jacques Fath offered cocktail drama in plummy rayon. Shown with an equally emphatic hat by Mr. John, a Hollywood milliner.

A devastating dater in screen-printed organdy as advertised by *Minx Modes, Jr.* in May 1951.

Demure after-five charm in black lace over lilac rayon, as advertised in Spring 1950. Update a vintage dress like this with black patent mules, and jeweled hair clips.

Glowing sophistication in gold Thai silk, sparked with Raj-inspired topaz pins at collar and pocket. Designed in 1951, this dress is timeless in its appeal.

From September 1955, waterfall flounces form a mock bustle on this stunning cocktailer by *Edward Abbott*.

For white-hot cocktail parties circa 1955, a *matelassé* dress designed to show the figure, with halter top and *pannier* overskirt. For dancing, this dress could be modified with side slits in the underskirt.

The hem dips in back, giving this 1960s prom dress natural swing. In lemon-lime charmeuse bound in pistachio grosgrain, on Kristi Talbert. Value: $35.00 — $55.00. *Author's collection.*

A *Tiny Bubbles* print dress in polished cotton, circa 1955. The bodice is boned for support; the skirt is reverse-pleated for swing. Value: $15.00 — $25.00. *Author's collection.*

A slice of lemon chiffon pie in dotted Swiss over taffeta, circa 1960. Elizabeth Haskett strolls the cottage gardens that grace *The Inn at Benecia Bay*. Value: $35.00 — $45.00. *Courtesy of Cheap Thrills*.

Elizabeth Haskett is queen of the prom, and princess of the piano in a 1960s dress of pink net with white-flocked dots. Value: $35.00 — $45.00. *Courtesy of Cheap Thrills.*

Pale blue polished cotton with a lacy bustier bodice for a junior miss dress worn by Jody Smith at *The Jefferson Street Mansion* in Benecia. Designed by Jessica McClintock, who still specializes in prom nights. Value: $35.00 — $45.00. *Author's Collection*.

You'll dream of dancing in this sweetheart frock of red cotton velveteen and star-spangled tulle, circa 1960, by *Lorie Deb*. Value: $35.00 — $45.00. *Courtesy of Lottie Ballou.*

On her, red chiffon with white polka-dots, a traditional prom gown by Jessica McClintock circa 1975. On him, red-and-white checked silk, a natty dinner jacket from the early 1960s. Value, dress: $45.00 — $65.00. Value, jacket: $55.00. *Author's collection.*

A rose by any other name could not be sweeter than Monica Moreno in this taffeta prom dress with ruffled hem and self-corsage, circa 1975.

Don't overlook a rhinestone-in-the-rough, just because the hem is torn or the trim is untidy. Simple sewing repairs can polish these pretty baubles from the 1930s-50s, when women weren't afraid to dress like girls in ruffles and lace, buttons and bows.

In blue-and-white eyelet, a spaghetti-strapped dater from the 1950s. Value: $35.00 — $55.00. *Courtesy of It's About Time.*

This skirt was salvaged from a 1930s deb dress of dove-gray Chantilly lace; hand-set rhinestones and hand-beaded crystal spark the hemline. As shown on Jamie Bradham, it's a sugary prom punch spiked with naughty black lace. Value: $35.00. *Author's collection.*

Take a Bow

A mock ribbon garter swoops down the skirt of this queenly linen dress. The ribbon ends in a swallowtail, extending below the hemline for a *trompe l'oiel* royal trump. Value: $55.00 — $65.00. *Courtesy of It's About Time.*

By noted couturier Robert Piquet, a 1950s strapless
stunner in lemon yellow with a black/white garter. A pouf
of ribbon at the waist echoes the short, puffy skirt.

A black and pink
diagonal swirl of
mock ribbon ties
this 1950s
sundress at the
left shoulder like
a big surprise
package.

Lisa Heigher lounges in a vintage circle skirt of hand-painted roses with self-crinoline, circa
1955. Value: $35.00 — $45.00. *Courtesy of Cheap Thrills.*

Circle Dance

The passion of Flamenco, captured in a cotton circle skirt from the early 1950s. The lace top is also vintage. Value, skirt: $25.00. *Courtesy of It's About Time.*

Bronze taffeta swirled with gold on a fancy skirt circa 1955. The gold top was salvaged from a 1930s evening gown. The copper cuff and earrings are by *Renoir*, circa 1960. Value, skirt: $25.00. *Courtesy of Cheap Thrills.*

A classic fruit motif bands a full cotton skirt from the early 1950s. This summery style is worn by Elizabeth Haskett at *Harlows'* in Sacramento.

Black faille with a starburst of rhinestones, circa 1955; the rhinestone necklace is from the same era. Value, skirt: $25.00 — $35.00. *Courtesy of Cheap Thrills.*

Christina Groves wears a schoolgirl cotton plaid dress from the 1950s, with retro saddle shoes — a great dance combo. Value: $15.00 — $25.00. *Courtesy of Cheap Thrills.*

Fish hang from an invisible line, styled after ancient Mesopotamian tile by way of *Melmac* dinnerware. Wear this cotton skirt with a turquoise tee and sandals. Value: $15.00 — $25.00. *Author's collection.*

Roses with a blue note dance on a cotton circle skirt with self-crinoline, a vintage delight for Katie Harris. Value: $35.00 — $45.00. *Courtesy of Cheap Thrills.*

Ricardo Salazar plays favorites, but Christina Groves gets her man, flaunting a Spanish dance dress with tiers of cotton and gold braid. Value: $25.00 — $35.00. *Courtesy of It's About Time.*

From darkest Africa, barkcloth
with a wood-block print outlined
in sequins. Value: $25.00 — $45.00.
Courtesy of Cheap Thrills.

This circle skirt swirls with a hand-painted golden motif borrowed from ancient Peru. Value: $35.00 — $55.00. *Courtesy of Cheap Thrills*.

Swing dancing is taught in special classes at most nightclubs, as shown with Western Swing style by Elizabeth Haskett and Matt Huey. Value, skirt: $15.00 — $25.00. *Courtesy of Cheap Thrills.*

This sleek pussycat adorns the oversized pocket
of a full felt skirt, made for a little girl by loving
hands at home circa 1955. Value: $15.00 — $25.00.
Courtesy of Cheap Thrills.

$\mathcal{W}$earing the $\mathcal{P}$ants

On Kristi Talbert, red velveteen slacks from the 1950s. The sparkly twin set is retro, the pearls are timeless. Value, slacks: $15.00 — $25.00. *Courtesy of Cheap Thrills.*

String of Pearls album cover featuring a swinging rope of those baubles. From a 1960s re-issue album cover.

A khaki slack set, for resort wear or lounging circa 1940. The plastic buttons in lettuce and tomato repeat the colorful braid trim. Value: $45.00 — $65.00. *Courtesy of It's About Time*.

It's OK to corral these 1950s jeans for the dance floor. Shown on Kristi Talbert with a bandanna-print halter top (not vintage). Value, jeans: $35.00. *Courtesy of Lottie Ballou.*

Elizabeth Haskett is coolly casual in a color-blocked rayon pantsuit by *Koret of California*, circa 1945. Did anyone say *bowling night*? Value: $55.00. *Courtesy of Cheap Thrills.*

Vintage pantsuits swing! This cool cotton print lounging set is by *Alice of Polynesia* circa 1960. Value: $35.00. *Courtesy of It's About Time.*

At the Improv

Steal the look of 1940s resort wear with baggy Bermuda shorts and shortalls, readily found at discount stores and consignment shops. Style this look for dancing with a silky blouse or lacy halter top, and strappy sandals or ballet flats.

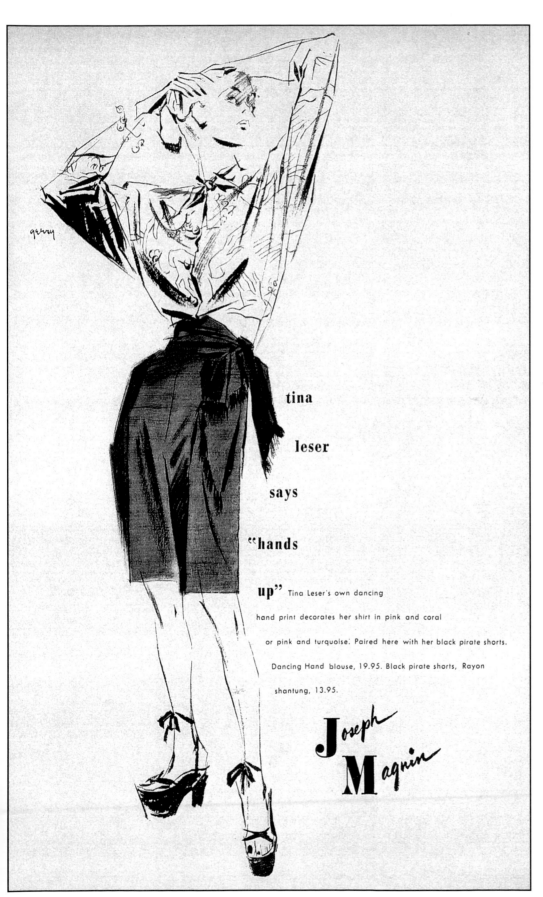

tina

leser

says

"hands

up" Tina Leser's own dancing hand print decorates her shirt in pink and coral or pink and turquoise. Paired here with her black pirate shorts. Dancing Hand blouse, 19.95. Black pirate shorts, Rayon shantung, 13.95.

Joseph Magnin

The real deal — black rayon shantung pirate shorts, by New York designer Tina Leser. As advertised by the *Joseph Magnin* department store in February 1946. The hands-on print blouse is worn with Calypso style.

Jamie Bradham strikes a perky pose in vintage jams and ruffled blouse. Both are polished cotton from the early 1950s. Value, each: $15.00 — $25.00. *Courtesy of Lotti0e Ballou.*

Cut a rug in this knickered jumpsuit of turquoise corduroy, circa 1955. Value: $45.00 — $65.00. *Courtesy of Lottie Ballou.*

Paisley corduroy Capris with matching crop top; a darling duo from the early 1950s. Value: $55.00 — $75.00. *Courtesy of Lottie Ballou.*

Capri pants in a vacation motif, circa 1960. Swing this look with pearly vintage heels from the same era. Value, pants: $25.00 — $35.00. *Courtesy of Luxe.*

Two little girls in peach are we! On the left, Elizabeth Haskett wears a candy-stripe organza sundress by *Jody of California*, from the 1960s. Her companion Amy Litteral wears a jacquard rayon confection by *Sergee*, from the same era. Value, each: $25.00 — $35.00. *Courtesy of Cheap Thrills*.

White rayon crepe
sundresses in a rag doll
print by *Judy 'n Jill*, as
advertised in February 1946.

This mid-1950s cotton sundress is pretty and practical for dancing. Value:
$25.00. *Courtesy of Cheap Thrills.*

You'll be *in the pink* when you dance in a light-weight denim dress like this one circa 1960. Value: $15.00 — $25.00. *Author's collection.*

They don't get any perkier than this 1960s shift with a cascade of yarn flowers. The A-line silhouette is flared enough for dancing. Value: $15.00 — $25.00. *Courtesy of It's About Time.*

Two floral shifts for resort wear *then*, for the dance floor *now*. As advertised by *Alex Colman* in October 1967.

Scenes from a Revolution-
ary War parade on a cotton
sundress by *Lanz of
California*. This was
probably a commemorative
style, honoring the nation's
Bicentennial (1776 to
1976). Value: $15.00 —
$25.00. *Author's collection.*

This polished cotton sundress with a short,
swingy skirt is typical of the early 1960s. Value:
$15.00 — $25.00. *Author's collection.*

Vintage sundresses were often paired with matching boleros, like this one in printed cotton from *Cole of California*. Two dance looks for the price of one! Value: $45.00. *Author's collection*.

Center left: Red, white and blue for a breezy nautical look from the early 1950s.

Bottom left: More seaworthy colors in a pinstriped sundress, as advertised in Spring 1951

A unique halter dress in a polished cotton print, with a peachy *Big Band*. By *Marion McCoy* circa 1960. Value: $45.00 — $55.00. *Courtesy of Cheap Thrills*.

From the flirty 1950s, a strapless sundress in sunny piqué. The bolero boasts topaz trim, and a scallop hem. Value: $55.00 — $65.00. *Author's collection*.

A big check print shows off *checker* buttons on this stylish vintage sundress by *Brigamce*.

The designer Claire McCardell showed this cotton sundress in fruit cocktail colors, for her 1951 resort collection.

That Ayres Look in a two-tier organdy print, as advertised in March 1951.

A double vision of *Ayres* as advertised in April 1950. The black cotton sundress gains sophistication from a matching jacket.

The New Separates

Great sock-hop style from *Koret of California*. This mid-1950s plaid skirt bears the *Everpleet* label for the company's patented process of topstitching at the hipline. Value: $25.00. *Courtesy of Cheap Thrills.*

Great Scot! A plaid kilt, sold at the *Best & Co.* department store for back-to-school 1959.

Play a little traveling music in mix 'n match cotton skirts. This early 1950s look comes alive with colorful broad-band belts.

Be a sweater (and skirt) girl with color-coordinated styles from 1951. For more youthful charm, add a charm bracelet and wear penny loafers.

Dots with Dash

Red and white polka-dot separates in wash 'n wear rayon, circa 1955. This playful set matches the mood of Nakkita Kient as she spoofs with her friend Derek Gouveia. Value: $45.00 — $65.00. *Courtesy of Cheap Thrills*.

On the left, white dots on gauze the color of a field mouse, circa 1945. The city cousin shows white dots on red rayon, circa 1955. Value, each: $25.00 — $35.00. *Courtesy of Lottie Ballou.*

A simple black and white dotted shirt-dress, as advertised in March 1946.

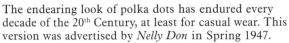

The endearing look of polka dots has endured every decade of the 20th Century, at least for casual wear. This version was advertised by *Nelly Don* in Spring 1947.

A dotty day dress from the late 1950s. Kristi Talbert trimmed the self-belt with *diamonte* clips from the mid-1930s. Value, dress: $45.00. Value, clips: $25.00. *Courtesy of Lottie Ballou.*

Polka dots are a background for Polka dancers on a vintage Lawrence Welk album cover. This folk dance from Eastern Europe joined forces with jive in the partnered movements of Western Swing.

— 4 —
Adornable You

Accessories have always been a powerful element of a woman's wardrobe, one that can make or break the look. With vintage clothing that *break* often occurs when the dress, shoes and accessories are *all* true to period. Remember, you're wearing vintage to look your best — not to win first prize at a costume ball. Here, we offer five rules for swing accessories, which should:

1. Allow for freedom of movement.

2. Highlight, and not distract from, your dance style.

3. Catch the light, be it strobe or electric, of the dance venue.

4. Reference the same mood as your clothing, not necessarily the same era.

5. Coordinate with your partner's costume, by color or era.

A clutch of shiny black beads are held securely on this expandable bracelet. Shown with an oversize metal brooch of a flower, complete with bobbing rhinestone pod.

A Shot on the Arm
One bold rhinestone bracelet is long on style, but expect a broad band of quality stones to set you back. These baubles, styled after the real thing worn by Hollywood stars and society ladies in the 1930s and 1940s, were pricey then and now but well worth it. Or, arm yourself with glitter on the cheap by piling on thin silver bangles. Preview the effect in *White Christmas*, when Vera Ellen struts a wrist-load while dancing at the cast party. (Tip: Old movies are a rich resource for how to wear vintage accessories).

For active dancing we commend the expandable bracelet. Usually a mad jumble of beads or sliced plastic, this style fits snugly on the wrist as held in place by elastic or spring action. But avoid charm bracelets, even though they capture a certain casual, All-American vintage style so perfectly. However, they're just too *jangly* for most swing dancing. (Tip: A link bracelet with engraved "ID" clasp or one bold charm makes a good substitute).

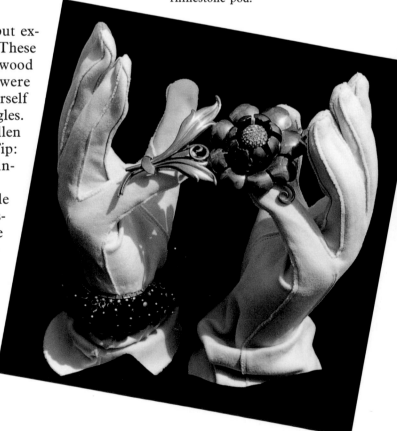

Getting Pinned

If you must wear a brooch, be sure the clasp is *very* secure. Otherwise, one spin may send it bouncing across the dance floor. (Tip: Pin the pin through your bra strap, or a scrap of cloth tucked inside the bodice of your garment, for security.)

Bold brooches held up to padded shoulders in the 1940s. Scatter pins were popular in the 1950s, and are a good alternative to the brooch.

Earlobe Lore

Jewelry sets were big in the 1950s, with earrings matched to a necklace, bracelet or both. But avoid chandelier earrings, as they may wind up swinging from the *ceiling* instead of you; instead, try studs or small hoops with retro style. (Tip: If your ears are not pierced then consider body art, with a makeup pencil or a *faux* tattoo, on the earlobe).

These rhinestone pins were advertised by *Trifari* in 1952, with matching clip earrings. If clips bother you, try converting them with simple safety pins, and wear them *scattered* on the bodice or collar of a vintage dress.

This white enamel and rhinestone summertime set by *Trifari* would look cool with a vintage cotton sundress, white patent sandals. Value: $35.00 — $55.00. *Author's collection.*

For an ethnic touch, try copper jewelry created in the 1950s by the Southern California jewelry firm *Renoir*. This three-part set packs a punch, in ombré red enamel over copper from the firm's *Matisse* line. Value: $55.00 — $75.00. *Author's collection*.

Crowning Glory

In days gone by, rhinestone bobby pins held up elaborate hairdos, while headbands smoothed down simple pageboys. These ornaments are popular again, and can be found in chain stores that cater to a youthful clientele. Many vintage clothing stores also carry them as a point-of-purchase display.

Don't forget to try a ponytail — unless your objective is the Lindy Hop, where one false aerial move might blind your partner! Top your tail with a chiffon scarf, satin bow, or silk flowers.

Having a bad hair day? A snood holds unruly locks in place, and is in keeping with the vintage mood. Snoods can be worn on their own, or under a hat. They're available in a wide range of colors at many vintage clothing shops. Or, wear a hat that can be removed for dancing.

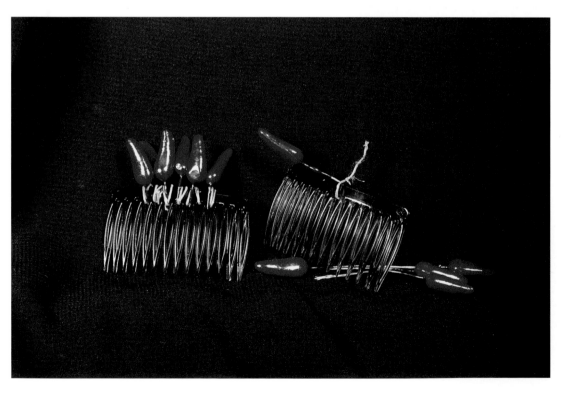

Jewelry can snag, and otherwise endanger your partner's health, if your swing style is energetic. In the alternative, try well-secured hair ornaments. Make your own *cherries jubilee* comb (or *chilies jubilee*, as shown) with supplies from any crafts shop.

Art Cajigas styles a 1940s updo for Andrea Pritchard, at the *Studio 28* hair salon in Sacramento. This lacquered and pinned style is a neat way to wear long hair.

The updo, from a 1940s advertisement.

Tuck a big silk flower behind your ear, and you're ready to bar-hop vintage style.

They were called *halo hats* in the 1930s, *picture h*ats in the 1940s and *sun hats* in the 1950s. By any name they were sweet, like this inexpensive craft store version chosen for its sunny disposition. Value, dress: $15.00 — $25.00. *Courtesy of Lottie Ballou.*

When the soft Fedora was first introduced into men's wear in the 1930s, it was considered a radical departure from the structured bowler, boater and top hats. But the new style quickly caught on, and became the headgear of choice by 1940. At its best worn on a tilt, as shown in this advertisement.

Footloose

Although the photographs of clothing in this book have been styled with all manner of footwear, in reality you should select sturdy shoes with good support. For example, when the Charleston became popular in the 1920s, manufacturers began advertising dance shoes with ankle straps and lower heels — for that same reason.

Women who have worn heels for years may protest that they are more comfortable than flats! However, a flat heel is essential for performing lifts and drops. You do the math: *Aerials + Heels = Sprained ankles.*

The sculptural style of ankle-strap dance sandals with jeweled toes, circa 1955.

The *Swing* shoe, as advertised in November 1936 with this enticing text: "Vanity presents its own version of this exciting new dance rhythm, light as a feather, giddy as to design."

Pandora touted a collection of *Lizard Jewels* throughout the 1940s.

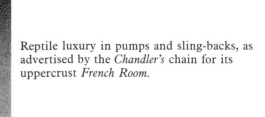

Reptile luxury in pumps and sling-backs, as advertised by the *Chandler's* chain for its uppercrust *French Room*.

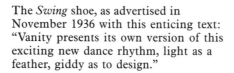

130

All Tied Up

Vintage men's clothing may be difficult to locate, especially when trying to match your partner's dance costume for a given style or era. This is when you can rely on accessories — and vintage ties are among the best! Ties are still available in a great array of silk and rayon, despite growing interest by collectors. Look for stylized Art Deco prints on wide ties from the 1930s, and bold hand-painted motifs on even *wider* ties from the 1940s.

Expect to spend anywhere from $5.00 to $75.00, depending on age, quality and rarity, at vintage clothing shops and shows. Of course, you can always join the flea market crowd. All but one of the ties shown here were collected by Tod Bedrosian of Sacramento, who vows that some of his best finds came from garage sales.

———————————————————————

Buffalo Gals Won't You Come Out Tonight? A whimsical silk-screened tie, sold by *Wembley* in the early 1940s.

Stylized silk flowers bloom on an array of silk ties from the mid-1930s.

An advertising rainbow of wide ties, for the 1940s *Esquire* man.

For Western Swing dancing, try a prickly *cactie* circa 1947.

A boy and his dog! John Saunders, age 11, sports a Golden Retriever silk tie. The pup is glowing in hand-painted silk circa 1945.

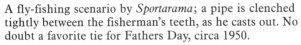
A fly-fishing scenario by *Sportarama*; a pipe is clenched tightly between the fisherman's teeth, as he casts out. No doubt a favorite tie for Fathers Day, circa 1950.

Hanky Panky

Pretty hankies aren't just for waitress uniforms anymore. Savvy collectors scoop up inexpensive hand-embroidered handkerchiefs by the handful, and so should you.

Tucked into the pocket of a sweet cotton frock from the 1930s, or pined onto the belt of a sundress from the 1940s, vintage hankies are a great accent when jewelry would be too clumsy on the dance floor.

Red roses on a blue-note hanky.

Two children in traditional garb
visit an oriental shrine, outlined in
colorful embroidery twist.

Luck be a Lady Tonight

When we spotted these recycled game pieces, they seemed just right for swing style. Artisan Deirdre Valdes collects vintage Mah Jong and backgammon tiles from the 1930s and 1940s, to string on elastic for snug-fitting bracelets (matching pins and earrings are also available). She recently began using Lucite dice from the 1950s and 1960s, adding vintage buttons and beads for variety. Expect to pay $60.00 — $100.00 for bracelets, $25.00 — $45.00 for other pieces.

These extra-long dominoes in butterscotch Bakelite, glowing from fond usage, find new life in the form of a cuff bracelet.

Mah Jong tiles in cheerful shades of Bakelite, joined by wooden buttons for a winning pair of bracelets.

A witty domino pin, the perfect size for lapel or pocket.

Mah Jong tiles in hand-painted bamboo, recycled as a lucky bracelet with matching earrings.

Beautiful Bakelite

Bakelite is a trade name coined in 1908 by its inventor, Dr. Leo Baekeland. He was a chemist who patented the first process for converting a resin made from carbolic acid and formaldehyde. Hardly the stuff from which a jewelry legend is born!

As it turned out, Dr. Baekeland had created a rock-hard substance that resisted heat and moisture, and was easy to mold. By the 1940s, his Bakelite Corp. was touting "the material of a thousand uses," which included novelty jewelry.

Bakelite jewelry was sold all across America — wherever colorful fruit and flower finery could be heaped into the bins of a display counter. Bakelite jewelry has attracted so much attention from collectors that a costume pin originally priced at $2.50 may now sell for $2500.00. Besides the fact that it's been priced sky-high. Bakelite jewelry is generally big and bold, too chunky for swing dancing.

Lucite is another alternative to Bakelite, as in this vintage bangle in transparent lime. Value: $15.00. *Author's collection*.

Quick 'n Easy Circle Skirt

The icon of circle skirts is the poodle! At *Cheap Thrills*, a vintage clothing shop in Sacramento, Marlene Davenport found the demand for these skirts impossible to meet. So, she began sewing a simple version herself, with a retail price of $25.00 — $35.00.

Marlene shares her basic skirt pattern and poodle template here. If you don't want a poodle, try other basic shapes. Siamese cats, ice cream cones, record platters and Coca-Cola bottles were all snipped from felt to decorate skirts in the 1950s.

This skirt should be cut from felt or heavy cloth; use pinking shears to save time on the hem and seams. The waist is just a doubled-over pocket for skirt-band elastic. (Tip: Yardage shops sell extra-wide elastic that avoids bunching, for this purpose.)

Nine-year-old Jamie Saunders wearing a lilac poodle skirt. Check out Jamie's *retro* crinoline, of a type available at vintage clothing stores for about $25.00. *Courtesy of Cheap Thrills.*

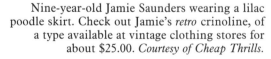

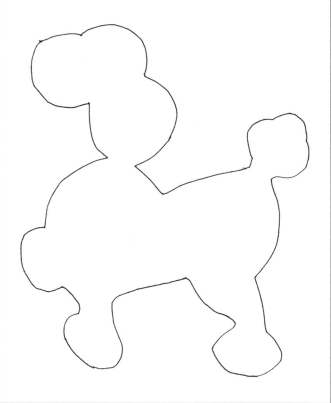

Enlarge at 150% to get approximate size.

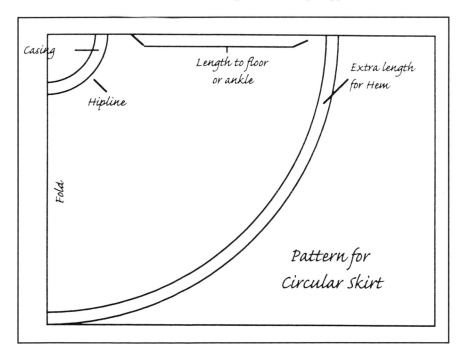

Casing

Hipline

Length to floor
or ankle

Extra length
for Hem

Fold

*Pattern for
Circular Skirt*

Circle Skirt

Cut the bottom template
from felt, the top from
poodle cloth (what else?).
You can add more texture
with bra©iding or cording.
(Tip: Use rescued rhinestone
bits or buttons for the collar;
apply gold braiding for a
glam leash.) For extra pizzazz,
cut a mini-poodle and stitch
it to the shoulder of a
cardigan sweater.

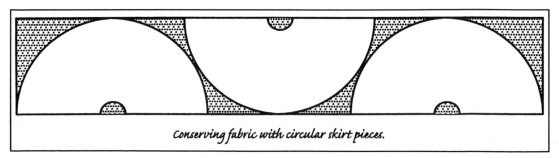

Conserving fabric with circular skirt pieces.

At the Improv

Throughout this book, we have offered ideas on mixing vintage with retro or contemporary clothing to create a great dance look. Here are more tips on how to maximize your vintage wardrobe with styling, sewing and salvaging.

Damaged goods are often marked down to *nothing* in vintage shop. Case in point, this 1970s strapless dress was tagged $10.00, due to underarm staining. The stains are out-of-sight and out-of-mind thanks to a retro mohair shrug.

This red taffeta crinoline is pretty enough to go solo. Topped by a vintage Chantilly lace bolero, with velvet banding and rhinestone buttoning. Value, slip: $15.00 — $25.00. Value, top: $25.00. *Courtesy of Cheap Thrills.*

— 5 —

Dance Contest

Swing music can't be beat for competitive dancing. Ricardo Salazar and Christina Groves are dance partners who travel to national competitions each year; he also teaches at the family-owned *Salazar Studios* in Sacramento, where the sudden popularity of swing dance has caused surging enrollment.

Many first-time students ask Ricardo to teach aerial moves on their first lesson, which is all but impossible unless they have a strong dancing or gymnastic background. New students should not expect too much in the way of air-born dancing for a while.

Although most Lindy Hoppers keep their feet on the floor, this dance incorporates aerial moves. Ricardo likens it to any other type of athletic endeavor: "It takes training and stamina on the part of both participants. Also, the right balance in body weight. It's supposed to look easy, but the man really needs to *hoist* his partner."

Ricardo and Christina show off their swing style here. Most of these dance steps have no formal name, since they are passed along visually from one dancer to another. Where names are shown, they are the ones most commonly used in swing vernacular. (Also, see Chapter 6 *Jive Lingo.*)

A graceful *dip*; don't make it a drop!

One, two, *ace-in-the-whole*.

Finger-popping *hepacats* approach each other in a dance routine.

Two views of a *'round-the-back* roll.

There are many variations on aerial *lift*s. An angled version is shown.

Ricardo wears retro slacks, suspenders and tie. Christina wears a schoolgirl shirtwaist, in crisp cotton plaid. Value: $15.00 — $25.00. *Courtesy of Cheap Thrills.*

Showing some *air* in a high-flying *lift*.

Swing it low, sister.

Another *ace-in-the-hole*, showing
the follow-through.

Practicing a new routine, front and back view.

The *lift-and-drop* in rapid sequence. This move is often used to end a routine.

She digs denim clamdiggers and a beaded cardigan from the 1950s. He pairs a vintage Hawaiian shirt with retro khaki pants. Value, clams: $35.00. Value, cardigan: $15.00 — $25.00. *Courtesy of Luxe.* Value, shirt: $45.00. *Courtesy of It's About Time.*

— 6 —

Jive Lingo

Vernacular speech or "slang" crept into common usage in the 1920s and soon became a hallmark of sophistication. Slang distinguished the city-bred *hepcat* from his mousy country cousin. Every trade and pastime had its own lingo, chief among them entertainment. Slang was so prevalent in the speech of jazz musicians, that it sometimes seemed as if they were speaking a foreign language.

Now you can get the inside scoop on jive lingo with the help of this little glossary. And for those who don't know *peau de soie* from *piqué*, we've included fashion terms.

Aerial: Dance step where the female partner is lifted into the air, before she is dropped back to her feet or on her seat. Usually dancing continues, with the aerial used as a segue into another portion of the routine.

A-line: Dress or skirt silhouette, flaring away from the body from bodice to hem.

Ace-in-the-Hole: Dance step where the female swings up and away from her partner; variation on a lift.

Air: The height achieved by the female partner during a lift.

Axe: Saxophone.

Bateau: Neckline, running from shoulder-to-shoulder in front and back, with a shallow curve.

Ballerina (a.k.a. Tea): Skirt length, falling to just above the ankle.

Be-Bop: Swing dancing to a rock-and-roll beat, popular with teen-agers in the 1950s.

Bell: Skirt silhouette, full at the hips and narrowing near the hemline. Generally, ballerina or knee-length.

Bent Note (a.k.a. Blue Note): A type of chording typical of swing and blues music. Given eight notes to the bar on sheet music, the seventh note is *bent* into a b-flat.

Cap: Short sleeve that just covers the top of the arm.

Capri: Narrow pants ending at mid-calf, originally made popular in the 1950s for resort wear on the Isle of Capri.

Cellulose: Man-made glucose distilled from the cell walls of plants, used for fibrous products including rayon fabric. A man-made cellulose distilled from wood pulp yields *viscose rayon*.

Chantilly: Delicate lace with floral designs on a hexagonal mesh.

Charmeuse: Lightweight, smooth fabric with a subtle sheen woven from silk, cotton, or rayon.

Chiffon: Lightweight, sheer fabric woven from silk, cotton, rayon or synthetics

Circle (a.k.a. Full): Skirt silhouette, very full and flared. Generally, cut from a 360-degree circle of fabric.

Couture: Fashion; French. High fashion is haute couture. A high-fashion designer is a couturier.

Crepe: Any fabric — but generally silk, wool or rayon that is heat-treated for a crinkly texture.

Crepe de chine: Crepe made from raw silk, woven with sheen. Lightweight and smooth in texture.

Crinoline: Plain cotton fabric with a low thread count, heavily sized (stiffened). Used so frequently for full slips, the term has come to mean any stiff, full slip.

Crystal: Very narrow pleating in a soft fabric (i.e., silk or chiffon). Alternatively, glass lead for superior color and clarity, used for beads and rhinestones.

Diamonté: Faux gems prong-set into fabric, or set into jeweler's metal as a decorative clip or buckle.

Dotted Swiss: Sheer, almost transparent cotton in any color, flecked with white dots.

Drop: Dance move where the female partner is dropped to her feet, or onto her seat.

Eyelet: Cotton or linen with a pattern of round "punched" holes bound with embroidery thread.

Faille (a.k.a. file): Silk or rayon fabric, with gentle horizontal ribbing.

Faux: Fake; French. In jewelry, this term references imitation gems.

Fichu: Froth of lace or crystal-pleated chiffon, usually white. Usually a decorative inset from neck to waist; may also be used as a cuff.

Georgette: Lightweight, sheer fabric similar to chiffon.

Grosgrain: A ribbed fabric or ribbon in cotton, silk or rayon.

Hepcat: Swing enthusiast, masculine.

Jams: Baggy shorts, ending just below the knee, popularized by surfers in the 1960s.

Jive: In swing parlance this term may refer variously to musical slang, dance steps or lifestyle. Modernly, may be derogatory.

Kitten: Swing enthusiast feminine partner of a hepcat.

Knife: Narrow pleating in a crisp fabric (i.e., cotton or linen).

Lamé: Fabric woven with metallic threads; often blended with silk or rayon to appear like cloth-of-gold or silver.

Licorice Stick: Clarinet.

Lift: Dance move where the female partner is lifted into the air.

Maquillage: Make-up; French.

Matelassé: Raised woven designs in any fabric, giving a blistered effect.

Moiré: Stiff silk or rayon fabric with a jagged pattern like a watermark.

Net: Stiff, heavy cotton or synthetic fabric with a low thread count and mesh-like weave.

Organdy: Crisp, sheet lightweight cloth woven from cotton or silk.

Ottoman: A stiff silk or rayon fabric with fairly large horizontal ribbing; see faille.

Pachuco: Members of a social-political movement among Hispanic males, originating in California during the 1930s and 1940s. Pachucos are loosely affiliated by their extreme style of dress, especially Zoot Suits.

Panache: Personal style; French.

Pannier: Basket; French. In fashion, this term refers to a skirt with wide sides, in the manner of hip bustles worn by noblewomen in the 1600s.

Parure: A matched set of jewelry. At least three items are needed for a parure. In the 1950s, generally a necklace, bracelet and earrings, but a pin or belt buckle may be added.

Peau de Soie: Skin-of-silk; French. Heavy satin with a dull lustre. Woven with a fine ribbing, but soft.

Piqué: Crisp cotton with a honeycomb weave, often used for cuffs and collars.

Platter: Vinyl record.

Portrait (a.k.a. Bertha): Romantic style of collar, deep and rounded.

Princess: Dress silhouette formed by long seams so the garment skims the body; no inset waistline.

Rayon: Man-made fabric from a glucose base of plant fiber, with good draping and dying qualities. A less expensive version (viscose rayon) made from a glucose base of wood pulp does not handle as well.

Response: Repeating or responding to another instrument as in Glenn Miller's "call and response" musical arrangements.

Retro: Modern version of a vintage style.

Rhinestones: Faux diamonds cut from glass or crystal. Generally clear with silver foil backing, although they may be tinted in pastel or iridescent shades with gold backing.

Silk: Originally from China, silk was brought to Europe in the 12th century as a luxury fabric. Soft and shiny, it drapes easily and dyes well. Depending on the weave, silk may be dense or sheer in weight.

Satin: Densely woven silk or rayon, with one lustrous side and one matte side.

Shantung: Silk or synthetic fabric with a rough, randomly slubbed texture.

Sheath: Dress silhouette in a straight or slightly-curved shape; no waistline.

Shorty George: A squatting stance with legs and arms.

Segué: Musical term for a bridge between two tempos, or two passages. In common usage, a physical motion that links two actions; or a written phrase that bridges two concepts.

Snood: Decorative hair net, used on its own or under a hat. Woven from silk or synthetic twist in any color to match or contrast with the hair.

Soutache: A type of trim achieved by stitching braid, cord or other thin goods in a scrolling pattern.

Swirl (a.k.a. Twirl): Swing enthusiast, feminine. So termed for the swirling movement of her skirt.

Taffeta: Crisp, lightweight fabric woven with a smooth finish made from silk, cotton, rayon or synthetics.

Thai: A type of silk woven with an iridescent lustre.

Trompe l'oiel: Trick-the-eye; French.

Tulle: A type of net with a sheer hexagonal mesh.

Twist: Heavy, shiny thread used for embroidery or the decorative treatment of clothing and accessories. Often fashioned of silk.

Velvet: Double-woven silk, cotton or rayon with a short and thick pile. Very plush and soft to the touch.

Velveteen: A form of velvet in single-woven cotton or rayon; less plush and soft than velvet.

Voile: Veil; French. A fine, sheer, lightweight fabric generally woven from natural fiber (silk or cotton).

Zoot Suit: A vintage style of men's wear (see pachuco). Suit trousers are cut high on the waist and wide in the seat; with deep front pleats and side pockets tapered below the knee, ending in cuffs. Suit jackets are wide-shouldered and double-breasted; cut to just below the seat, with deep venting.

— 7 —
Call and Response

We don't pretend that this resources guide is comprehensive, but at least it's a start in the *right-on* direction. These are all stores where we found great stuff, in a range of prices. (Of course, you can always make an offer; we're not talking *Macys* here.)

Where available, the owner's name is listed for your convenience in making telephone inquiries. Or try the nearest antiques row near your residence, where such clothing is often sold in specialty booths and shops.

Vintage Resources Guide

American Rag Clothing
150 So. La Brea Avenue
Los Angeles, CA ZIP
(323) 935-3154

A large emporium with high turn over, offering all manner of men's and women's vintage clothing from the 1940s forward. Especially good for *funky chic* garments and accessories. Good prices; call in advance to find out if there's an in-store special. The Los Angeles location is the largest. Also check it out in San Francisco at 1305 Van Ness Avenue.

Cheap Jack's Vintage Clothing
841 Broadway
New York, NY
(212) 777-9564

The East Coast version of *American Rag*, with an even larger inventory. So sad, but *Jack's* is not so *cheap*. Also, the lay-out is a bit confusing, since many of the best items are whimsically hung from the ceiling and sales help must assist you to look. Still, this store is a must stop for any vintage clothing enthusiast visiting the Big Apple.

Cheap Thrills
1217 21st Street
Sacramento, CA 95814
(916) 446-1366
Contact: Marlene Davenport

Now here's a store name that's a model of truth in advertising! This was probably the first store in Sacramento to specialize in vintage clothing. (Really, it's vintage shops inside a converted, purple-painted house.) *Cheap Thrills* specializes in women's clothing; front-hall neighbor *"Uncle Freddy"* has a good selection of men's wear.
The new owner, Marlene Davenport, keeps her shop overflowing with standard stock like 1940s rayon dresses and 1950s prom dresses, plus a full line of retro accessories. There's also the occasional great find like a designer gown, or a pristine gabardine suit; truly a *cheap thrill*.

Cherry
185 Orchard Street
New York, NY 10002
(212) 358-7131
Contact: Cesar Padilla

Tucked along a side street near the trendy watering holes of SoHo, *Cherry* is a convenient starting point to outfit yourself in retro duds for a night on the town. A small store, but well-stocked in sexy glad rags and accessories for men and women. Also, groovy swimwear from the 1950s and high-tech jewelry from the 1960s. Look for the occasional designer label vintage gown.

Crossroads Trading Co.
1901 Fillmore Street
San Francisco, CA 94115
(415) 775-8885

One of the first buy-sell-trade stores still operating at the original location in San Francisco. An inexpensive mix of 1960s and 1970s, with some earlier pieces, of clothing, shoes and accessories. This store has grown into a California chain with locations in Oakland, Sacramento and San Jose (also Seattle, Washington).

Deirdre Valdes & Co.
2141 "E" Street
Hayward, CA 94541
(510) 582-5902
Contact: Deirdre Valdes

This is an artisan jewelry company that features bracelets and other items fashioned from vintage Bakelite and Lucite game pieces. Dierdre Valdes has jewelry stocked in several stores across the Bay Area, including a prestigious museum gift shop. (See Chapter 4, *Adornable You*.)

Funky Furnishings
4945 Folsom Boulevard
Sacramento, CA 95819
(916) 456-2905
Contact: Chris Cloud

A fun store brimming over with clothing, furniture and amusing icons of the American lifestyle circa 1950 — 1970. Great pickings for the inveterate bargain hunter.

Golyester
136 South La Brea Avenue
Los Angeles, CA 90036
(323) 931-1339

One of the first vintage emporiums, still an invaluable source for unique clothing and funky accessories. The emphasis is on women's clothing from the mid-20th century but you'll also find outrageous shoes, plastic handbags, Bakelite jewelry, swim wear and lounge wear. A special section of the store offers a wide range of dress and drapery fabric from the 1940s.

It's About Time
2104 "J" Street
Sacramento, CA 94814
(916) 446-5944

This is another landmark of vintage style in Sacramento. Owner Jeri Sparks began in the trade as a "picker," working thrift shops for rayon shirts and cotton dresses. Now she offers a large selection of clothing, with the occasional beaded flapper dress or Victorian opera cape. There's also a good selection of vintage hats, shoes and jewelry.

Lottie Ballou
130 West "E" Street
Benicia, CA 94510
(707) 747-9433
Contact: Margo Adams

A treasure trove of quality vintage clothing, tucked discreetly at the end of a sleepy street stemming from the tourist center of Benecia. You'll find a wide range of women's dresses, gowns and suits along with accessories, especially hats and shoes. Look for bargains in jewelry ranging from Victorian garnets to Bakelite bangles, and matched sets in rhinestone and crystal.

Luxe
2453 Lombard Street #104
San Francisco, CA
Contact: Lis Normoyle

Luxe carries a wonderful and diverse inventory of women's clothing from the 1940s — 1960s. Owner Lis Normoyle designed a line of clothing for her own Melrose Avenue boutique, some 30 years ago and she's known among her colleagues as having "one of the best eyes in the business." Look for clean-cut gabardine suits and jackets; unique cocktailers and evening gowns; cashmere sweaters, and Hawaiian shirts. Other specialties are new\old stock granny shoes; boxy leather handbags and pristine bag\shoe sets in alligator. *Luxe* sells by appointment and at shows only. Although the goods are all top-quality, you can make any reasonable offer.

Right to the Moon, Alice
240 Cooks Falls Road
Cooks Falls, N.Y. 12776
(607) 498-5750
Contact:Alice Lindholm

Now we're letting away a trade secret – this is where high-end vintage clothing vendors on the East Coast shop, for *their* best bargains! A diverse inventory of well-made women's garments, with the occasional designer label. Lots of prom dresses and evening gowns, suits and dresses, fun summertime stuff and some accessories.

Trixie's Vintage Boutique
1724 Fillmore Street
San Francisco, CA 94115
(415) 447-4230
Contact: Trixie Neff

You'll love this store, if only to chat about a girl's best friend — vintage clothing, of course — with the well-versed and friendly owner Trixie Neff. Her shop is small but packed with goodies. Look for dresses, cocktailers, gowns, shoes, jewelry and handbags. The overall look is trendy but not funky. Prices are reasonable, with some real bargains.

Ver Unika
148 Noe Street
San Francisco, CA 94114
(415) 431-0688

This is cutting-edge vintage with a good inventory of radical men's suits and shirts from the 1960s – 1970s. For the distaff set, *Ver Unica* specializes in retrofitted cashmere sweaters and twin sets. There are also lots of high-end suits and cocktail dresses in top shape. Two husband \wife teams own the store, and work hard to keep the inventory well-stocked.

Wasteland, The
1660 Haight Street
San Francisco, CA 863-3150
www.thewasteland.com

During the height of hippie style, this was *the* store to shop. As at *Crossroads*, there's a lot of buy-sell-trade going on, so the inventory turns over rapidly. The flagship San Francisco location still has hippie lustre, located in a gaudily gothic building in the heart of Haight-Ashbury. Great bargains on the cute and funky are standard stock, with a large selection of denim jeans. You may also find designer garments from the 1930s — 1970s. There's a bit of everything in accessories: handbags, shoes, hats and some jewelry (vintage plus retro). *Waste-land's* sister store is 7428 Melrose Avenue in Los Angeles, has a similar inventory.

Of course, you can also have fun searching for the type of vintage duds that will suit your *swing style* at flea markets and garage sales, thrift shops and consignment shops. Don't forget to look for *retro* clothing at chain stores that cater to a youthful clientele like *Gap, Express, Guess, Rampage, Wet Seal, Clothestime* and *Target*.

If you want a truly custom look, or you're into competition dancing, check out the companies that make new clothing and accessories with vintage style. Some are listed below; you can also cruise the web (check out www.Thread Baron.com) or inquire at a local dance studio. These retro duds are all available by mail-order or website with catalogs upon request.

Retro Resource Guide

Art's Shoes
13023 100th Ave. N.E.
Kirkland, WA 98030
(425) 814-9191

A specialty business owned by Art Bog-osian, who began making shoes in his native Armenia in 1970. When he moved to America in 1979 he began specializing in dance shoes, and now his line of *Hand-crafted Ballroom Shoes* is sold by his catalog and at dance studios, nationwide. These are shoes for serious dancers. There are some two dozen styles for women, all with low- or medium-height heels. Many are open-toed, and most feature ankle-straps or T-straps for security. For the men, about a half-dozen Oxford styles, and a spectator wing-tip in white saddle with black, gray, brown or navy trim. Expect to pay just over $100.00 a pair (but for the spectator, which runs $185.00).

ReVamp
321 Linden Street
San Francisco, CA 94102
(415) 863-8626

Retro clothes can be quite amusing, and true-to-form, as shown in this duo from ReVamp. The blcak overalls for her, and the suit vest with slacks for him, are circa 19455.

You should send for this store's catalog just to see their limited-edition recreations of day wear, cocktail dresses and evening gowns in a range of natural and blended fabrics. This is mostly women's clothing, with a few items for their partners, but no shoes or accessories. Women's blouses sell for about $50.00, jumpers for about $85.00, with day dresses in the $100.00 range. There's a good selection in "The Evening Gown Collection," which includes gowns styled in the pre-jazz Belle Époque era; these run from $125.00 — $250.00. Men's slacks are about $100.00, shirts and vests are in the $50.00 — $60.00 range. *ReVamp* will soon issue "The Swing Collection" for "hepcats and their kittens."

Siegel's Clothing Superstore
2366 Mission Street
San Francisco, CA 94110
(415) 824-7729
www.zootsuitstore.com

This is a family-owned business with a large selection of men's *retro* clothing and accessories, including Fedoras. Ask for their help in styling your Zoot Suit, since accessories are the whole key to this look. That is, suspenders are worn in lieu of a belt; a long, gold watch-chain may be clipped to the waistband. Ties are wide and short, and large handkerchiefs are often tucked into the jacket. *Siegel's* own line of *Towne Square Slax* are cut in the baggy zoot-style from a modern rayon blend. The company just added a *Retro-Wear* private label. Their manufacture is supervised by an 80-year-old head tailor, using the store's original patterns from the 1930s. Depending on your choice of fabric, expect to pay $30.00 — $100.00 for a pair of slacks, $25.00 to $100.00 for a shirt, and $175.00 — $400.00 for a suit.

Bibliography

These are a few of my favorite fashion resources. (Of course, my own book is included!) Sadly, many of these books are out-of-print, but I've listed them anyway since they may be available through your local library or used bookstore. If you are truly inspired, look for vintage *Vogue* and *Bazaar* fashion magazines at clothing shows and stores, dating back to the Swing Era. Even the ads are a great resource!

Houck, Catherine. *The Fashion Encyclopedia*. New York: St. Martin's Press. 1982.

Ley, Sandra. *Fashion for Everyone: The Story of Ready-to-Wear, 1870s-1970s*. New York: Charles Scribner's Sons. 1975.

Milbank, Caroline Reynolds. *Couture: The Great Designers*. New York: Stewart, Tabori and Chang. 1985.

Mulvagh, June. *Vogue History of 20th Century Fashion*. New York City: Viking; London: Penguin, Inc. 1988.

O'Hara Callan, Georgina. *Dictionary of Fashion and Fashion Designers*. London: Thames and Hudson, Ltd. 1998.

Reilly, Maureen. *Hot Shoes*. Atglen, PA: Schiffer Publishing, Ltd. 1998.

Smith, Pamela. *Collecting Vintage Fashion and Fabrics*. Brooklyn, NY: Alliance Publishers. 1995.

_____. *The Swing Era*. New York: Time-Life Records, Inc. 1970.

Index

MORE SCHIFFER TITLES

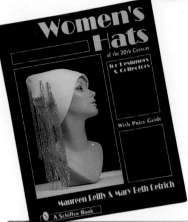

Women's Hats of the 20th Century For Designers and Collectors Maureen Reilly & Mary Beth Detrich. Hundreds of beautiful hats by important American and European milliners, all illustrated in over 550 color photos. This carefully researched book profiles the creators and lists the most desirable designer and salon labels. It offers special sections with tips on dating, evaluation, and storing and decoration, as well as a useful value guide.

Size: 8 1/2" x 11"   570 color photos   240 pp.
Value Guide
ISBN: 0-7643-0204-3   hard cover $49.95

Hot Shoes One Hundred Years Maureen Reilly. Explore women's shoes as a powerful talisman of fashion, culture, and sexual energy. With 500 original color photographs and two dozen vintage illustrations, this book tells the real history of shoes real women wore. Each photo caption includes a value range.

Size: 11" x 8 1/2"   540 color photos   224 pp.
Price Guide/Index
ISBN: 0-7643-0435-6   hard cover $49.95

Vintage Fashions for Women 1920s-1940s Kristina Harris. Over 400 photographs of fun, sophisticated, frivolous, and glamorous fashions on live models. Evening gowns, beaded dresses, classic suits, knickered and skirted bathing suits, distinctive cloche hats, beaded bags, elaborate shoes, and a host of accessory items are included with anecdotes and historical details to convey a vivid picture of the styles of the Jazz and Big Band eras. Specific information on construction, value, and date make this a great book for collectors and designers alike.

Size: 8 1/2" x 11"   403 color photos   192 pp.
Value Guide
ISBN: 0-88740-986-5   soft cover $29.95

Wearable Art 1900–2000 Shirley Friedland & Leslie Piña. From one-of-a-kind hand-made accessories to commercially-made apparel, wearable art has become important for vintage and contemporary fashion. Showcasing over 500 color photographs, an extensive illustrated glossary, bibliography, and value guide, this is the first book to cover both vintage and new wearable art creations, presenting a compelling topic at its best. It will delight all with interests in fashion and art, the unusual and the beautiful.

Size: 8 1/2" x 11"   512 color photos   208 pp.
Price Guide
ISBN: 0-7643-0719-3   hard cover $49.95

50s Popular Fashions For Men, Women, Boys & Girls Roseann Ettinger. Those swinging Fifties are fondly remembered in this bright, eye-catching book of everyday fashions for men, women, boys and girls. Color photos illustrate hundreds of examples, most of them never worn and retaining their original colors and freshness. A glossary, index and price guide make this a very useful book for collectors.

Size: 8 1/2" x 11"   633 color photos   160 pp.
Price Guide
ISBN: 0-88740-724-2   soft cover $29.95

Schiffer books may be ordered from your local bookstore, or they may be ordered directly from the publisher by writing to:

Schiffer Publishing, Ltd.
4880 Lower Valley Rd
Atglen PA 19310
(610) 593-1777; Fax (610) 593-2002
E-mail: schifferbk@aol.com

Please visit our website catalog at *www.schifferbooks.com* or write for a free catalog. Please include $3.95 for shipping and handling for the first two books and 50¢ for each additional book. Free shipping for orders of $100 or more.

Printed in China